ANALYZING
CLIMATE
CHANGE

ASKING QUESTIONS, EVALUATING EVIDENCE, AND DESIGNING SOLUTIONS

PHILIP STEELE

Cavendish
Square

New York

Published in 2019 by Cavendish Square
Publishing, LLC, 243 5th Avenue, Suite 136,
New York, NY 10016

Cataloging-in-Publication Data

Names: Steele, Philip.
Title: Analyzing climate change: asking
questions, evaluating evidence, and
designing solutions / Philip Steele.
Description: New York : Cavendish Square,
2019. | Series: Analyzing environmental
change | Includes glossary and index.
Identifiers: ISBN 9781502639387 (library
bound) | ISBN 9781502639394 (pbk.) |
ISBN 9781502639400 (ebook)
Subjects: LCSH: Climatic changes--Juvenile
literature. | Global warming--Juvenile
literature.
Classification: LCC QC981.8.C5 S834 2019 |
DDC 551.6--dc23

Produced for Cavendish Square by
Tall Tree Ltd
Editors: Jon Richards
Designers: Ed Simkins

Printed in the United States of America

CONTENTS

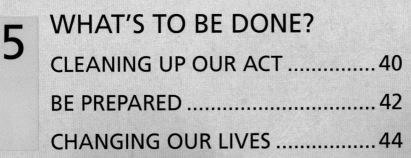

IT'S TIME TO TALK ABOUT CLIMATE CHANGE

For people on Earth, our home planet seems like a familiar place. We see the seasons come and go. Every now and then we experience a thunder storm, a rough sea, a heatwave or a blizzard. We catch fish and grow crops, just as our grandparents did before us. In some ways, the patterns of our lives continue much in the same way as they have done for centuries.

People take to the streets of Paris to protest against climate change in 2014.

"This Earth is our only home. Together, we must protect and cherish it."

Former UN Secretary-General Ban Ki-moon

AN UNKNOWN FUTURE

But how secure is our future? In the last 50 years, scientists have found that the surface of our planet is overheating. The climate is changing. This theory has been met by dismay and disbelief. Even so, the evidence for it has grown. It is now accepted as a fact by scientists around the world, and nearly all of them agree that this change is anthropogenic – caused by human activity.

The age-old patterns of climate and weather are changing fast. This matters because the future of life on Earth, no less, depends on our understanding of the problem and the actions we take. What might happen and what is to be done?

DROUGHT

Prolonged dry periods, or droughts, can damage crops, leading to hardship for farmers and societies that depend on farming for their income.

DISEASE

With the world warming, tropical diseases that were linked to regions close to the equator, such as malaria, may spread into temperate parts of the world.

GLACIER RETREAT

Warming conditions have seen many of the planet's large glaciers retreat. This one is on the slopes of Mount Rainier, USA.

STORMY WEATHER

As moisture levels and energy increase in the atmosphere, conditions will become more volatile, leading to stronger and more frequent storms.

The world's climate is changing, and opinions differ as to what or who is responsible. In each chapter of this book we'll look at different aspects of climate change, exploring and discussing the issues involved. There are vital issues to examine and questions to be raised and discussed.

Let's talk about them...

WHAT IS CLIMATE?

Some days may be rainy or dry, while others may be sunny or cloudy, or hot or cold. These are the weather conditions at any one time. Climate is the standard pattern of weather recorded in a place or a region over a much longer period, from around 30 years up to hundreds or even thousands of years.

Clouds of condensed water vapor pass over the blue waters of Lake Pukaki in New Zealand.

LAND AND LIFE

Physical geography, such as high mountain ranges or the distance from the sea, may affect the climate of a region. Climate decides the kinds of plants and animals that live in a region. In turn, those plants affect the climate. A region that shares similar life forms is called a biome. If the climate of that biome changes, some species may become extinct.

6

THE WIND AND THE RAIN

Our climate includes all sorts of variations, which interact with each other. Temperature, air pressure, winds and ocean currents all play their part.

The air around our planet is called the atmosphere. It is made up of various gases. One of these is water vapor, which is formed when water in seas or lakes evaporates. The warm vapor cools as it rises, and condenses to form droplets of water. These join together to fall as rain or freezing snow, a process called precipitation. The rain falls and drains into rivers, lakes and oceans, and the whole water cycle starts again. Any changes to the water cycle affect our lives.

The water cycle is the continuous movement of water through Earth's atmosphere and ground.

Clouds

Evaporation

Precipitation

Runoff

Groundwater

Sea

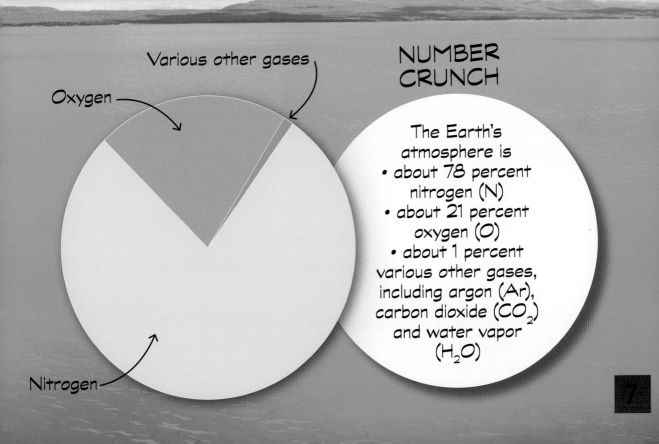

Various other gases

Oxygen

Nitrogen

NUMBER CRUNCH

The Earth's atmosphere is
- about 78 percent nitrogen (N)
- about 21 percent oxygen (O)
- about 1 percent various other gases, including argon (Ar), carbon dioxide (CO_2) and water vapor (H_2O)

WHY DOES CLIMATE CHANGE?

The Earth's climate has always been changing. For many millions of years the planet has generally been cooling, while temperatures have swung between very cold extremes (ice ages) and warmer periods in between (interglacials). The last great Ice Age ended about 11,700 years ago. Even during these major swings, there were sometimes smaller, shorter and localized switches in the climate.

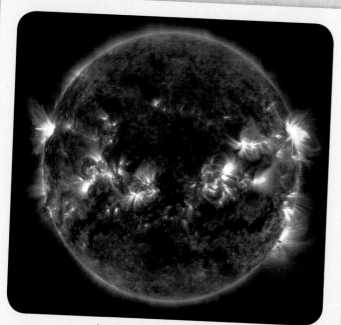

ACTIVE STAR

The Sun is a huge ball of burning gas where atoms are fused together under enormous temperature and pressure. This fusion produces massive amounts of energy and radiation.

NATURAL CHANGES

Many natural events can force Earth's climate to change. Earth's orbit, the path it follows around the Sun, sometimes changes slightly. The angle of Earth's axis as it spins also changes slightly. Both of these variables affect the amount of radiation the planet receives from the Sun. Periods of great volcanic activity release massive clouds of ash, which may block out the Sun's heat and light for a time. The growth of plants and forests reduces the amount of CO_2 in the atmosphere.

RAYS FROM THE SUN

The amount of radiation given out by the Sun, our nearest star, varies from time to time. This can make Earth become warmer or cooler. Changes in the gases of Earth's atmosphere also affect the amount of the Sun's radiation received by the planet.

THE NEW THREAT

Natural climate change in the past has mostly been gradual, but there have been rapid changes too. Natural changes are of course still happening today, but they are interacting with a new warming that seems very different. It is sudden and extreme, and it is linked to the way in which humans are treating the planet on which they live.

NUMBER CRUNCH

Core samples of Antarctic ice up to 2 miles (3 km) in depth may be about 800,000 years old. They contain tiny air bubbles. Scientists can study these to work out what CO_2 levels were long ago and how they have varied over time.

In 1991, Mount Pinatubo in the Philippines erupted and threw up so much dust that it blocked sunlight and reduced global temperatures by 1°F (0.5°C) for two years.

ATMOSPHERE AND CLIMATE

It is the warmth and light of the Sun that make life possible on Earth. The gases in Earth's atmosphere (see page 7) also help us, by screening out harmful radiation. They are essential to life. Life-giving oxygen is breathed in by animals including humans. Carbon dioxide is absorbed by plants and trees. Water vapor gives us the most precious liquid on the planet: water.

GREENHOUSE GASES

Some gases in the atmosphere are called greenhouse gases. Their presence in the atmosphere, along with the water droplets in clouds, helps to keep our planet warm. Without them, the Earth would be too cold to inhabit. Important greenhouse gases include carbon dioxide (CO_2), methane (CH_4) and nitrous oxide (N_2O).

NUMBER CRUNCH
The average temperature of Earth's surface is about 59°F (15°C). Without greenhouse gases, it would be about 0°F (-18°C).

Greenhouse gases, including water vapor, trap energy from the Sun and stop it from escaping into space. This warms the atmosphere.

MAKING THE CONNECTION

Before the 1800s, scientists had little idea about past changes in the climate. From the 1820s onwards, they began to find out about the part played by gases in warming the planet. They realized that the balance of gases in the atmosphere directly affects the climate. Some began to question what would happen if that balance was upset. Was climate change solely a natural process, or was it also affected by human activities?

OXYGEN PROVIDERS

Plants absorb carbon dioxide and use sunlight to turn it into sugars, which they then use to produce energy. At the same time, they release oxygen into the air.

LET'S THINK ABOUT...
GREENHOUSE GASES

- are naturally present in the atmosphere.
- help to keep Earth warm.
- protect life on Earth.

- are emitted by human activities.
- can overheat Earth if there is too much of them.
- can put life on Earth at risk.

1 EARTH AND SUN

Our climate is created by the Sun. This fireball, a gigantic nuclear reaction, is nearly 93 million miles (150 million km) away from Earth. It pumps out energy in the form of electromagnetic radiation. Some of this radiation, such as light, we can see with our eyes. Special equipment can also trace other forms of radiation, such as infrared and ultraviolet light, radio waves or X-rays, and measure changes in our climate.

As much solar energy is absorbed by the atmosphere in one hour as the world's entire population uses in a whole year.

EARTH IMPACT

When the Sun's energy hits Earth, about one third of it is reflected straight back into space, either by the atmosphere or by the planet's surface. The rest is absorbed by Earth and its oceans, so the planet heats up.

NUMBER CRUNCH

The Sun has been radiating energy for about 4.6 billion years. In about 3.5 billion years' time it will become so hot that Earth's climate will not be able to support life. In about 4.5 to 5.5 billion years, it will collapse.

BOUNCE-BACK

As Earth heats up, it begins to radiate energy itself, mostly in the form of infrared rays. Some infrared rays pass freely out into space, but some are trapped by the greenhouse gases and reflected back to the surface. This greenhouse effect makes Earth even warmer. If more greenhouse gases are released into the atmosphere, then more infrared rays are blocked and the overheating begins.

TAKING THE TEMPERATURE

The temperatures of Earth's surface can be measured directly by thermometers at weather stations around the world. Ships can be used to measure sea surface temperatures. Temperatures can also be worked out indirectly, for example by using satellites to measure infrared radiation from the planet's surface.

GLOBAL GREENHOUSE

Greenhouse gases in the atmosphere trap energy from the Sun, helping to warm the planet.
1. Radiation travels through space from the Sun and is absorbed by Earth.
2. Some of the Sun's energy is reflected back out into space.
3. Some gases in the atmosphere trap the energy and reflect it back to Earth, where it warms the planet up even further.

LET'S THINK ABOUT...
THE SUN'S RADIATION

- makes life on Earth possible.
- drives our climate.
- may be balanced by greenhouse gases.

- is naturally variable.
- may be made more intense by greenhouse gases.
- may overheat the planet.

1 OVERLOAD

Humans unknowingly started to have an impact on the world's climate in the 1700s and 1800s, when they brought in new ways of farming and producing goods. They built factories with tall chimneys that poured smoke into the atmosphere. They built railways, locomotives and steamships. Thousands of people moved into big cities, with homes heated by coal fires. Buildings and countryside became covered in grime and soot.

POWER POLLUTION

Many power stations burn fossil fuels to heat water. This produces steam which spins turbines to produce electricity.

FOSSIL FUELS

The 1900s saw new roads, millions of cars, air travel and new power stations which only added to the problem. The fuels that made this new developed world possible were coal, oil and gas. They were created from living matter that died millions of years ago, and so are often called fossil fuels.

Plumes of smoke pour into the atmosphere from forest fires in Thailand in this photo taken from orbit. These fires release huge amounts of carbon dioxide.

14

RAMPING UP THE CARBON

When fossil fuels are burned, they release carbon dioxide. Since the year 1750, the amount of CO_2 in the atmosphere has increased by 40 percent. The biggest increase has happened in recent years, with CO_2 emissions rising sixfold since 1950. Fossil fuels make up 87 percent of human emissions, other industrial processes make up 4 percent, and changes in land use, such as cutting down forests, make up 9 percent.

The increase in CO_2 emissions has made the greenhouse effect more intense, trapping more heat in the atmosphere. Each decade since the 1980s has been hotter than the one before. Can this be a coincidence?

DEFORESTATION

Deforestation plays a large part in the increase in carbon in Earth's atmosphere. Cut-down trees can no longer absorb carbon dioxide and they will release the carbon in their trunks when the wood is burnt. This photo shows a clearing in the Pantanal region of Brazil.

NUMBER CRUNCH

In 2012 it was reported that coal, oil and natural gas produce most of the world fossil fuel emissions.
Coal: 43 percent
Oil: 36 percent
Natural gas: 20 percent

LET'S DISCUSS... FOSSIL FUELS

- have powered our modern way of life.
- have been used to create new materials such as plastics.
- have made it easy to travel round the world.

- emit carbon dioxide when burned.
- have polluted land, sea and air.
- have been a major cause of global warming.

Natural gas

Coal

Oil

GLOBAL WARMING ARGUMENTS

The debate about global warming has raged over the last 30 years. Some say that the man-made global warming theory is a hoax. But the evidence has stacked up the other way.

QUESTION IT!
IS IT A MYTH THAT HUMANS ARE CAUSING GLOBAL WARMING?

HASN'T CLIMATE CHANGE been happening naturally for millions of years? Why blame humans when there could be all sorts of other rational explanations? Couldn't all this be part of long-term natural cycle, perhaps a 'blip' on the way to another Ice Age?

SOME PEOPLE, including some scientists, politicians and journalists, oppose the climate change theory. They claim that the data is incorrect or deliberately fiddled with. They say that the human connection is not proven.

NATURAL CAUSES MIGHT include sunspots — the darker, cooler marks that appear on the face of the Sun from time to time. These are caused by magnetic fields and show that the Sun's radiation is naturally variable.

"Twenty-five years ago people could be excused for not knowing much, or doing much, about climate change. Today we have no excuse."

South African Archbishop Desmond Tutu, winner of the Nobel Peace Prize, in 1984

AREN'T RECENT HIGH TEMPERATURES and drought the result of a natural variation in the temperature of currents in the Pacific Ocean, a cycle known as the El Niño effect? What does that have to do with CO_2 emissions?

SCIENTIFIC STUDIES SHOW that the chances of recent temperature rises being solely due to natural causes are minimal to non-existent. This is something that 97 percent of leading scientists agree with.

THE EL NIÑO EFFECT is indeed natural. Not all events are caused by carbon emissions, although they may be affected by them.

A REVIEW OF SUNSPOT HISTORY in 2015 confirmed that such activity on the Sun's surface is not a significant cause of global warming or cooling.

The People's Climate March took place in New York City in 2014. It was the one of the largest ever marches in support of urgent climate change policies.

17

THE EVIDENCE

In the 1890s, a few scientists were already predicting there would be trouble with CO_2 emissions. During the 1960s, worries began to grow, both about air pollution and about the greenhouse effect. Many ignored the warnings, including those with interests in the oil industry. But the real picture became clearer in the 1970s.

CHANGING TIMES

The science of climate change is very complicated and is breaking new ground. Some of the earliest climate scientists were often being challenged and criticized. But during the decades that followed it became clear that these really are unusual times. Temperatures are rising rapidly and records are being broken.

This map shows which parts of the world have become much warmer over the last 100 years.

2012
Temperature difference 1912–2012

-4   -2   0   2   4
Fahrenheit

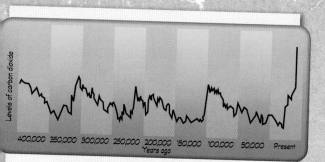

Levels of carbon dioxide

400,000 350,000 300,000 250,000 200,000 150,000 100,000 50,000 Present
Years ago

RISING LEVELS

This graph shows the levels of CO_2 over the last 500,000 years, with a sharp surge in recent times. This surge has coincided with an increase in global temperatures since the end of the 19th century, as shown by the graph on the right.

HOTTER AND HOTTER

The planet's ten hottest years since formal records began were all recorded in the last 12 years. All major studies tell much the same story. Since 1900, the Earth's average temperature has warmed by about 1.53°F (0.85°C). This may not sound like much, but even small rises can be enough to destroy entire ecosystems.

TELL-TALE SIGNS

All other indicators of global warming are closely monitored and tell the same story. The oceans are warming and becoming more acidic as they absorb CO_2. Arctic ice is melting. Sea levels are rising. A whole range of equipment, from satellites in space to buoys in the ocean, is giving us a better global overview than ever before.

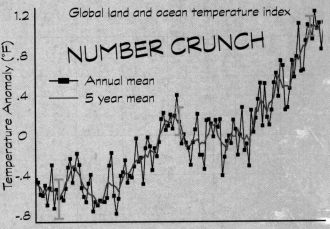

Global land and ocean temperature index

NUMBER CRUNCH

■ Annual mean
— 5 year mean

Temperature Anomaly (°F)

1.2 .8 .4 0 -.4 -.8

1880 1900 1920 1940 1960 1980 2000

In 2016, it was found that changes in sea level in the Pacific Ocean could be used to estimate future warming. Researchers correctly predicted that by the end of 2016 the surface would be 0.5°F (0.3°C) hotter than in 2014.

LET'S DISCUSS...
CLIMATE SCIENTISTS TODAY

• have satellites, computers, accurate equipment.
• have a global reach to monitor the climate.
• can work out past climatic conditions fairly accurately.

• must work with great urgency.
• face future conditions that remain unknown.
• often face political and corporate opposition.

19

SILLY SEASONS, WEIRD WEATHER

The statistics on global climate change may seem glaringly obvious. But because the climate takes in many local differences and influences, it is sometimes hard for people to work out exactly what is going on in their own backyards. If they have just experienced an unusually snowy winter or a cold, wet summer, they may be tempted to question whether global warming exists at all.

THE BIGGER PICTURE

The reason of course is that climate scientists are generally referring to average temperatures worldwide, not to local weather. While people are throwing snowballs in New York, southern Africa may be suffering from an unusually long drought, lasting for years.

As energy levels in the atmosphere get higher, the weather may become increasingly difficult to predict and storms may become more powerful.

SPRING FLOWERS
The blooming of flowers on cherry trees indicates the start of spring in many countries.

BIRDS AND BEES
Not all indicators of global warming are extreme or violent events. Plants and animals sensitive to temperature are having to adapt or disappear from some places. Changing seasons may add to the many problems that already affect crops and migrating birds and insects which pollinate plants, such as bees. Even the fate of small animals and plants may be of huge importance to us all. Any gardener can recognize 'season creep.' In northern lands, spring is arriving 2 to 3 days earlier each decade, while autumn is later by 0.3 to 1.6 days.

STORMS AND FLOODS
Global warming does not mean that we all experience nicer weather. Some areas become more rainy, because warm air can hold more water vapor. There will be more floods in some places, but more drought in others. Weather events may be more stormy and unpredictable.

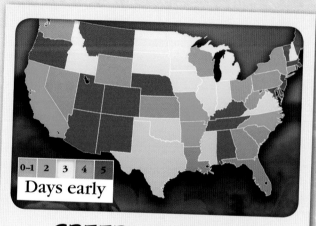

0–1 2 3 4 5
Days early

CREEPING SPRING
This map from 2010 shows how many days earlier spring started in each state compared to the period from 1961 to 1980.

LET'S THINK ABOUT...
GLOBAL WARMING

- is global but not always local.
- may temporarily benefit some regions.
- is part of an even bigger picture.

- may be disastrous for some regions.
- will affect the whole world of nature.
- humans are part of that world.

2 IS CLIMATE CHANGE HAPPENING?

A number of climate events seem to buck the trend when it comes to global warming. Critics often claim that these disprove the whole theory. Do they – or is the truth more complicated than that?

SEA ICE AROUND parts of Antarctica has not been shrinking as it has in the Arctic Ocean. In recent years, NASA satellite images have actually shown some record-breaking seasonal ice coverage in the Antarctic. Surely if the Southern Ocean was becoming warmer, the sea ice would have melted as predicted?

HURRICANE KATRINA devastated the US state of Louisiana in 2005. It killed at least 1,245 people, possibly many more. It caused $108 billion worth of damage. At the time, many people were quick to blame climate change for this disaster, but since then isn't it true that no scientist has been able to prove that this was the case?

ANTARCTICA
is different from the Arctic in that it is occupied by a large landmass. Overall, the southern continent is losing ice. The recent expansion of sea ice may have been caused by regional wind patterns, or by a natural temperature switch in the eastern Pacific Ocean.

HURRICANES
like Katrina are extremely complex storms. Pinpointing the blame for such an event is really difficult, but scientists are learning more all the time. They may not have a simple yes or no answer, but they can ask: 'Was the storm made more likely by human-linked climate change?' and 'Was it made more severe?'

QUESTION IT! SOMETIMES THE EVIDENCE JUST DOESN'T STAND UP, DOES IT?

HUMAN-LINKED warming is often just one of many factors affecting our climate. Solar activity and variations in the Earth's orbit also contribute to the warming.

This satellite image shows the swirling storm clouds of Hurricane Katrina. It formed over the Bahamas on August 23, 2005, and lasted 8 days.

CLIMATE MODELLING

If climate science is complicated, trying to predict the future impact of global warming is even more so. Yet that is what we have to do if we are to tackle the problem and prepare ourselves. Throughout history, humans have tried to forecast or influence weather and climate, sometimes using religious rituals or prayers, sometimes by observing the natural world. Today, we have powerful computers.

DATA CRUNCHERS

Climate models are ways of predicting future climate conditions or effects, using mathematics. They are based upon the laws of physics and chemistry. They use data from many different sources to simulate the interactions of atmosphere, oceans, land surface and ice. They can factor the levels of radiation from the Sun. Climate modelling can be linked to other areas of modelling, such as land use.

NUMBER CRUNCH

Climate modelling suggests that by the end of this century the global temperature will have increased between 2°F (1.1°C) and 11.5°F (6.4°C). The most likely estimates are between 3.2°F (1.8°C) and 7.2°F (4°C).

WEATHER SATELLITES

From their position high above the atmosphere, weather satellites can study atmospheric events over a larger area, helping meteorologists predict the weather.

HOW RELIABLE?

Today's computers can process mountains of data, but models are still only models. They are only estimates of future trends, and cannot predict events with any certainty. They are not long-range weather forecasts. However, if separate climate models match up in their findings, then it does make their predictions more probable.

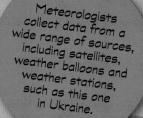

Meteorologists collect data from a wide range of sources, including satellites, weather balloons and weather stations, such as this one in Ukraine.

TIPPING POINT

Climate does not always change exactly when scientists would expect. It has a tendency to resist change and stay steady until it reaches a final tipping point. Then one little factor can cause rapid change, such as the loss of Arctic permafrost releasing trapped methane, which increases warming and causes further loss of the permafrost.

LET'S THINK ABOUT... CLIMATE MODELLING

- can bring together vast amounts of data.
- applies mathematical and scientific principles.
- can help us plan for the future.

- is only as good as the data it uses.
- needs constant updating to stay relevant.
- may not be an accurate prediction.

MELTING ICE AND WARMER OCEANS

The impact of global warming will depend on the actions we take now and on how much the temperatures actually rise. There are many unknowns, but much of the scientific research will focus on the Poles and the oceans, which play such a big part in the world's climate patterns.

An iceberg floats in the Arctic waters near Greenland. As glaciers melt, huge chunks break off and float out to sea as icebergs.

THE BIG THAW

The permafrost, the deep-frozen soil near the Arctic, is melting. As vegetable matter thaws, it releases large amounts of methane into the atmosphere. This greenhouse gas is about 30 times more powerful than CO_2.

RISING SEAS

Higher temperatures cause land ice to melt and the water in the oceans to expand. As a result, sea levels are rising quickly. Some scientists predict a rise of 2.6 feet (0.8 m) to 6.6 feet (2 m) by the year 2100. Already, small islands in the South Pacific have begun to disappear. Even the lower estimates would cause coastal flooding, storm surges and coastal erosion. Flooding from the sea may cause salt to enter fresh water supplies in coastal regions. As the oceans absorb more CO_2 they become more acidic (see page 19), damaging coral reefs and marine life.

TAKING MEASUREMENTS

Scientists on a ship in the Arctic Ocean lower sensors into the water to measure temperature, salinity and levels of carbon.

LAND ICE, SEA ICE

Greenland's thick ice sheet is warming quickly and seasonal melting is increasing. Meanwhile the extent of summer sea ice in the Arctic is shrinking. At the other end of the planet, Antarctica's ice sheet overlaps the coast, forming ice shelves. These may break up into massive icebergs as the oceans warm.

LET'S DISCUSS...
IF THE ARCTIC SEA ICE MELTS

- it no longer reflects back into space 50 percent of the solar radiation it receives.
- the Arctic Ocean absorbs more heat from the Sun.
- neighboring landmasses become much warmer.
- marine, polar and tundra habitats are damaged.
- easier human access opens up the Arctic to oil drilling.
- Industrial development would release more greenhouse gases.

WET OR DRY?

Water sustains life on the planet. How climate change will affect water over the next hundred years is going to be vital. In some dry areas, water shortages may increase by 30 percent. The old patterns of animal migrations, sowing and harvesting, wet season and dry season may be disrupted. Unpredictable weather makes survival harder.

FUTURE RAIN

For each 2°F (1°C) of temperature increase, the water vapor in the atmosphere increases by about 7 percent. Exactly how this plays out in a changing climate is still uncertain, but global warming increases the likelihood of problems. It is probable that wet regions of the world will become wetter. In some places, rainfall may be less common, but more intense. Heavier rainfall often results in flooding and erosion of river banks. Although water is needed to grow crops, too much of it can also destroy them.

FUTURE FLOODING
As rainfall levels become less predictable, we may see increases in extreme weather events, such as this flooding in Ho Chi Minh City in Vietnam.

During dry months, the lack of water can turn forest floors into a tinder box, where the slightest spark can cause raging fires.

DRY AS DUST

Drought, long periods of dry weather, may have several natural causes. It may also be associated with the effects of climate change, which may also make droughts longer and more extreme. Dry areas of the world may become drier. If plants die, then there are no roots left to trap moisture in the soil. Whole regions may turn into hot desert or dustbowls. As temperatures rise, wildfires may become more common. Fires increase CO_2 levels in the atmosphere, and destroy the forests that soak up carbon.

DROUGHT

With little water in the ground, the earth cracks and is unable to support crops and other plants, leading to hunger and even famine.

LET'S DISCUSS...
WATER

• sustains the forests that soak up CO_2.

• makes the Earth a planet of life.

• controls the global climate.

• shortages are already common and may become worse.

• floods may become widespread and more severe, threatening animal and plant species.

HUMAN IMPACT

The rise in CO_2 emissions has happened at the same time as the number of humans on our planet has grown. That's no coincidence. About 7.4 billion people now live in the world, seven times more than in 1804. By 2100, it could be 11.2 billion, according to the United Nations. The population is peaking at a time when the climate is in crisis.

The Nile flows through several African countries. Ten of these countries have partnered through the Nile Basin Initiative to develop the river in a cooperative manner.

NUMBER CRUNCH

About 23 percent of the world's population lives on or near the coast — at a time of rising sea levels.

23 percent

PROBLEMS AHEAD

The human cost of climate change could mean loss of farmland and entire low-lying islands to the sea, and water supplies becoming too salty to use. Climate refugees may have to migrate to other lands. Climate change places a strain on the production of food and access to water. Already, nations compete for scant water resources in dry regions of the world. Could shortages lead to conflict?

INTERNATIONAL ACTION

Poor people in underdeveloped regions of the world will be the first to suffer. However, climate does not recognize national borders. All regions and all nations will need to adapt and to cooperate with each other.

> "There is no scenario in which the risks to financial assets are unaffected by climate change. That is just a fiction."
>
> Prof. Simon Dietz, London School of Economics, 2016

RISK TO LIFE

Rising temperatures generally bring an increase in deaths or illnesses caused by the heat. The World Health Organization states that climate change is likely to affect the ways in which infectious diseases are passed on. Warmer climates could see increases in the numbers of mosquitoes which spread malaria (below).

MALARIA
Some mosquitoes spread malaria when they bite a human host, passing the disease directly into the blood.

ECONOMIC MELTDOWN?

The economic costs of climate change could be world-changing. Storm damage, flood defenses, crop failure or insurance pay-outs already cost a fortune. Economists have estimated that climate change issues could knock between $2.5 trillion and $24 trillion off the value of world financial assets.

LET'S DISCUSS... CLIMATE CHANGE

- can be met with positive action.
- means we must all work together.
- can be prepared for.
- impacts every human on the planet.
- could put lives in danger.
- carries big economic and political risks.

31

3 A QUICK FIX?

The worst possible impacts of global warming are catastrophic. Even the least bad impacts are not good. Surely these problems are preventable? Or are we all doing too little, too late?

HUMAN INGENUITY OVERCOMES most problems, doesn't it? After all, we can send spacecraft to travel beyond our Solar System. If the impact of climate change is so bad, surely we can meet this challenge?

QUESTION IT! SURELY THERE ARE WAYS TO FIX THIS?

DOES IT MAKE SENSE for us to cut back on industrial development that will benefit future generations, just because of climate change? That development may produce new technologies needed to protect our planet.

International agreements now propose that we reduce greenhouse gas emissions. Won't that solve the problem? If not, why are we doing it?

Kiribati in the Pacific is made up of more than 30 low-lying islands and is home to more than 100,000 people. These islands could be lost to rising sea levels.

THE MOST important thing is to tackle the problem at source by reducing fossil fuel emissions. Will that provide a solution? Not immediately. Even if we limit the temperature increase to 3.6°F (2°C), the warming will continue to affect everyday life for many years. Even if the climate stabilizes, sea levels might continue to rise for long into the future.

THERE MAY BE technological fixes, but they won't be quick or simple. Complicated problems may need multiple approaches. Doing nothing is not an option. Global warming is already happening and it is serious.

AT HIGHER temperature levels, the momentum becomes almost unstoppable. Climate effects may last for hundreds or even thousands of years.

4

CLIMATE ACTION

Green politics, centered upon the environment, became popular in the 1970s. These ideas spread to many countries. In the 1990s, more and more people protested against global warming, fossil fuels, oil companies, new airports and shale gas extraction or fracking. Activists asked people to work out how much carbon their activities used up, such as a holiday flight. This was called their carbon footprint.

OPPOSITION

At the same time, a movement grew up in opposition, claiming that climate change was a hoax. Powerful politicians and journalists argue that climate change is not taking place. US President Donald Trump, for example, has vowed to end what he calls the 'war on coal.'

The Greenpeace ship, Rainbow Warrior, arrives in Israel to protest at the building of a coal-fired power station.

GREENPEACE

PARIS2015
UN CLIMATE CHANGE CONFERENCE
COP21·CMP11

UN SUMMITS

In 1988, the United Nations and the world's governments at last started to take action. They formed the IPCC and in 1992 organized a conference in Rio de Janeiro, Brazil, known as the first Earth Summit. It was attended by 172 governments and many members of NGOs (non-governmental organizations). In 1997 in Kyoto in Japan, 37 industrial nations agreed a protocol to reduce greenhouse gas emissions. This was challenged by the oil industry and by many politicians. Despite many obstacles, the Paris Climate Conference of 2015 (known as COP21, left) signed up to a target for limiting temperature increase.

NUMBER CRUNCH

The Paris Agreement of 2015 aims to keep temperature increases well below 3.6°F (2°C), aiming for 2.7°F (1.5°C). This could mean zero emissions are reached between 2030 and 2050.

LET'S DISCUSS...
THE PARIS AGREEMENT OF 2015

- agrees to keep temperature increases below 3.6°F.
- targets 2.7°F.
- aims to combat climate change.

- has yet to be fully ratified (approved).
- will need enforcement before it can work.
- may have come too late because emissions are still at a level that will cause many problems.

4 PUTTING ON THE BRAKES

It is hard to get countries to agree on curbing greenhouse gases. Their economies may depend on carbon-intensive industrial development, such as car manufacturing, logging or mining. Their politicians may have elections to win tomorrow, not in 20 years' time. The public who vote for them may be more worried about their paycheck than about some complicated climate theory.

ENERGY TRANSITION

When countries do agree to sign up to climate action, what steps can they take? In 2010, Germany, one of the world's leading industrial nations, decided to reduce greenhouse gases by 80 to 95 percent over 40 years. They planned a big switch to renewable energy (see pp. 40–41). They put money into researching energy efficiency and energy conservation.

SUN AND WIND
Switching from fossil fuels to renewable sources, such as solar and wind, will greatly reduce emissions. Today, nearly 24 percent of all electricity is generated using renewable sources.

POLICY OPTIONS

Governments can pass laws regulating companies and limiting the emissions from factories, power stations or motor vehicles. They can put a tax on fossil fuels. They can try to ensure more absorption of CO_2 by planting large areas of forest, which will act as a carbon sink. Climate laws need to be enforced or they are pointless. Illegal logging continues in many parts of the world.

CARBON TRADING

The Kyoto Protocol of 1992 brought in CO_2 emission allowances or quotas or for each country. These can be traded on the 'carbon market.' A country that wants to emit more CO_2 can purchase spare quotas from a country that uses less.

NUMBER CRUNCH
(absolute emissions)

1 China
28 % of total

2 USA
16 %

3 India
6 %

4 Russia
5 %

5 Japan
4 %

Logging in many parts of the world has cleared large areas of forest. Despite having protected park status, this forest in Thailand was cleared by illegal logging in 2015.

LET'S THINK ABOUT...
VEHICLE EMISSIONS

- must be tested in the factory.
- must be tested in all vehicles on the road.
- can be limited by traffic zoning in cities.

- tests have been falsified, and may not be reliable.
- are responsible for 26 percent of greenhouse gas emissions in the USA.
- may be coming from 2 billion cars on the world's roads by 2035.

4 UNEVEN FIGHT

The fight against climate change needs international cooperation. It also needs a lot of money to pay for flood defenses or investment in new technologies. But who should be paying? Are the world's least developed countries, often those least responsible for CO_2 emissions, getting a fair deal?

AREN'T THE TROPICAL REGIONS and small islands that are the most at risk from violent storms, sea level rise and drought generally areas of low income and poor infrastructure? They mostly have low greenhouse gas emissions.

OVER HALF OF THE COUNTRIES with the highest CO_2 emissions are the ones least at risk from the effects of climate change, aren't they?

Thousands demand action on climate change in London in 2014. The protest followed news that the world's CO_2 levels were becoming dangerous and irreversible.

QUESTION IT!
IS THERE ONE LAW FOR THE RICH, ANOTHER FOR THE POOR?

HOW HELPFUL IS IT TO TAKE HISTORY into account when settling the bill for climate change? Do modern states in Europe and North America have a moral responsibility for the actions of their ancestors? After all, the industrialists of the 1800s knew little about the environmental damage they were causing.

WELL, THE WEALTHIER countries do recognize the problem and in 2009 agreed to provide $100 billion a year to help the less developed countries meet the challenges. Insurance companies are also agreeing to help developing countries cover themselves for losses caused by natural and climate-change related disasters.

THERE ARE INJUSTICES within nations, as well as internationally. The richest in society have the biggest carbon footprint, for example by driving big cars or flying frequently. The poorest in society get hit the hardest, as they lack the economic resources to deal with flooded homes or moving to a new area. Is that fair?

EVEN SO, PROBLEMS REMAIN. Poorer countries point out that some of the international assistance comes in the form of loans or investments that will benefit the rich countries. Much of the money that has been pledged has yet to be paid. Others point out that the costs are rising all the time and that support needs to be increased and extended over a longer time scale.

5 CLEANING UP OUR ACT

All proposed climate action comes back to the same basic question. What's to be done about the carbon problem? We already have ways of controlling CO_2 emissions, of removing them, and of not making them in the first place. The technology is speeding ahead.

CARBON BUSTERS

There are various ways to remove CO_2 waste from power stations or other industrial plants and to store it deep underground. However, carbon capture and storage is expensive. Ways are now being found to suck CO_2 from the atmosphere as well, but the costs of that technology would be very high.

70%

NUMBER CRUNCH

China increased its solar power installation 13-fold between 2011 and 2015. Its solar power production is 70 percent of the world's total.

WIND POWER

Wind turbines turn the energy of moving air into electricity. Today, they produce about 4 percent of the planet's total electricity.

LET'S DISCUSS...
SAVING ENERGY

- by turning off lights and appliances in homes, schools and offices.
- by insulating houses from heat loss.
- by driving less and using more public transportation.
- by making sure cars are fuel-efficient.
- by generating power locally, avoiding loss along transmission lines.
- by recycling materials in the home.

THE RACE FOR RENEWABLES

Can renewables effectively replace fossil fuels in electricity generation? This issue is much debated, but wind, solar or water (hydrolelectric, tidal or wave) are making rapid advances. The game is changing quickly, with improved energy storage and the development of so-called smart electricity grids that can deal with variations in input. Instead of huge nuclear, oil, gas or coal-fired power stations, we may in the future see many smaller local schemes, with houses and even roads that generate their own clean power.

ELECTRIC CARS

Zero-carbon electric cars can now perform well and operate safely. Battery recharging still limits distances and extends time, but again, the technology is advancing year by year. Traffic jams pumping toxic fumes into the air may soon be thing of the past.

While electric cars can reduce emissions in cities, they still require electricity, most of which is produced by fossil fuels.

5

BE PREPARED

As well as planning a clean-energy future, we must prepare cities, the countryside, coasts and homes for the impact of global warming. How and where do we build new housing? How do we manage water supplies? How do we protect threatened wildlife species? The decisions are often tough ones to make.

These floating homes near Seattle, Washington, are designed to rise and fall with changes in the water level, so that they don't flood.

FLOOD DEFENSES

In the Netherlands, Delta Works is a project that protects coasts and estuaries with a long network of barriers, dams and dikes. Defending low-lying land and cities against flooding and storm surges has been going on for centuries. In many countries, this will be increasingly necessary as sea levels rise. Houses are being designed to rise and fall with changing water levels, to stop them from being flooded.

NATURAL BARRIERS

Construction is expensive, so in many places dunes and reefs will have to provide a natural barrier, while some areas of land will have to be abandoned to the sea. Tropical islands are often protected by coastal mangrove forests. Where these have been destroyed, the flooding could be disastrous.

NUMBER CRUNCH

The number of people affected by river flooding around the world could triple to 20 million by 2030.

FLOOD BARRIER

The Thames Barrier in London was completed in 1982 and has several large barriers which can be closed to prevent rising waters from flooding the city.

FORESTS – AND FIRES

Planting trees and other plants in dry lands helps to create moisture and shade and prevents the spread of deserts. In Egypt, a forest is actually being grown in the desert, using waste water diverted from sewers. Forests also absorb CO_2 emissions. In regions such as California and Australia, hotter weather means more forest fires, and forests will need careful management with firebreaks to protect homes.

LET'S THINK ABOUT...
IN CASE OF FLOODING WE CAN

- plant more trees.
- avoid paving over gardens to stop water running off too quickly.
- improve drainage and gullies.
- safeguard our homes.
- check local flood defenses.
- look out for flood warnings.

5 CHANGING OUR LIVES

Whatever our attitudes now, climate change is a fact and it is already happening. The human experience in the rest of this century will shape our experience. It may test us to the limit and we need to work together.

IS CLIMATE CHANGE a case of corporations putting profit before the good of the public? Have oil and gas companies ignored the evidence, covered up the truth and lobbied politicians in order to keep the oil and the money pouring in?

IS CLIMATE CHANGE purely about the science, or is it about political policies? Have some parties on both the left and right of politics believed that economic growth is more important than safeguarding the environment for future generations?

"Earth has enough resources to meet people's needs, but will never have enough to satisfy people's greed."
Mohandas K Gandhi, 1869-1948

QUESTION IT!
IS THE REAL PROBLEM ABOUT HOW WE LIVE OUR LIVES?

WHY DO SOME PEOPLE like to blame human beings for everything and apologize for being alive? We should be proud of our technical skills and our business skills and making a better life for ourselves.

IS GLOBAL WARMING a story about how we live our lives? We have all wanted more and more material goods, entertainment, faster travel and instant communication. Yet we have lost touch with the natural world, treating it as a commodity rather than our home.

WILL WE BE THE FIRST generation to leave our children a less developed world to inherit? We cannot put the clock back to a pre-industrial age. We will solve climate problems as we have solved problems before.

WELL, IT COULD BE SAID that it is global warming that is likely to spoil our children's future. If that was created by humans, then we have a moral duty to change the way we use the planet.

GLOSSARY

ABSORB
To take in or soak up energy (or a liquid) by a chemical or a physical process.

ACIDIC
Containing acid. For example, rainwater may become acidic if mixed with polluting gases.

ANTHROPOGENIC
Refers to pollution caused by human activity, often with reference to climate change.

ASSETS
A useful or valuable possession. The value of most assets is affected by climate change.

ATMOSPHERE
The envelope of gases surrounding a planet.

BIOME
A large natural community of plants and animals living in a major habitat, such as a rainforest.

CARBON CAPTURE
A method of capturing carbon from its source point, such as the chimney of a fossil fuel power plant, to prevent it polluting the atmosphere.

CARBON FOOTPRINT
The amount of CO_2 released into the atmosphere as a result of the activities of a person or company.

CARBON SINK
A forest, ocean or other natural environment that can absorb CO_2 from the atmosphere.

CLIMATE
The weather conditions in an area over a long period of time.

CLIMATE MODELS
A computer model that simulates weather patterns, used to predict future climate change.

COMMODITY
A raw material that can be bought and sold.

CONDENSE
Change from a gas or a vapor into a liquid.

CONSENSUS
A general agreement, such as when scientists agree on the factors that contribute towards climate change.

DUSTBOWL
Land where the soil has turned to dust as a result of drought or poor farming methods.

ELECTROMAGNETIC RADIATION
A kind of radiation including visible light, radio waves, gamma rays, and X-rays. The Sun emits electromagnetic radiation.

EMISSION
The release of gases or pollutants into the atmosphere, particularly when fossil fuels are burned.

ENERGY CONSERVATION
Reducing energy consumption by deliberately using less fuel or electricity.

ENERGY EFFICIENCY
Minimizing the amount of electricity or fuel used.

EROSION
The wearing away of something by wind, water or other natural processes.

EVAPORATES
To change from a liquid into a vapor.

EXTINCT
Of a species of plant or animal that no longer has any living members.

FIREBREAK
A gap in vegetation, such as a ditch or a road running through a forest, that acts as a barrier to slow the progress of a fire.

FOSSIL FUELS
A natural fuel such as coal or gas, formed millions of years ago from fossilized living organisms.

FRACKING
The injection of liquid at high pressure into underground shale rocks in order to release oil or gas.

FRESH WATER
The non-salty water on Earth's surface, found in glaciers, icebergs, ice sheets and rivers.

GREENHOUSE EFFECT
The trapping of the Sun's heat in the lower atmosphere, causing global temperatures to rise.

GREENHOUSE GAS
A gas that contributes to the greenhouse effect by absorbing radiation. CO_2 is a greenhouse gas.

GRIDS
Networks of power lines that deliver electricity from the power station to the consumer.

HUMAN RIGHTS
Rights that belong to every individual person, and which are protected by law. For example, the right to live is a universal human right.

HYDROELECTRIC
Generating electricity from the power of moving water, such as from a dam. The water turns turbines to generate the electricity.

ICE AGES
Long periods of low global temperatures, resulting in an extension of polar ice sheets and glaciers.

ICE SHELVES
A thick floating platform of ice that forms where a glacier or ice sheet meets the coastline.

INFRARED
Invisible electromagnetic radiation with a wavelength greater than that of visible light. Heated objects emit infrared radiation.

INTERGLACIAL
A period of warm temperatures, lasting thousands of years, that separates the glacial periods within an ice age.

MIGRATE
To move from one region of the world to another in search of better living conditions or to escape poverty, war or famine.

NUCLEAR REACTION
A process in which two nuclear particles collide, producing something different from the original particles. Inside the Sun, hydrogen atoms fuse to create helium, releasing huge amounts of energy.

PERMAFROST
A layer of soil just beneath the Earth's surface that stays frozen all year round.

POLLINATE
To transfer pollen to the female reproductive organs of a plant, allowing fertilization.

PRECIPITATION
Rain, snow, sleet or hail that falls to the ground.

PROTOCOL
The rules governing the affairs of state. Alternatively, the original draft of a treaty agreed to in a conference.

QUOTAS
A fixed share of something that a person or group is allowed to receive, or must contribute.

SEASON CREEP
Observed changes in the timing of the seasons, such as when spring starts sooner each year.

SUNSPOTS
Areas of cooler surface temperature on the Sun's surface that appear as dark spots. Their distribution can affect temperature on Earth.

TEMPERATE
A region or climate with mild temperatures.

TIPPING POINT
The point at which an accumulation of small changes becomes enough to cause a more significant change.

WATER CYCLE
The cycle in which water evaporates from rivers and oceans and returns to the Earth's surface in the form of rain or snow.

ZERO-CARBON
Causing no release of CO_2 into the atmosphere. For example, a zero-carbon home would burn no fossil fuels and get its energy from renewable sources, such as solar and wind.

INDEX

PICTURE CREDITS